*Healing through faith,
forgiveness...*

# HOPE & LOVE

PAUL KRAUS

Published in Australia by
Coventry Press
33 Scoresby Road
Bayswater VIC 3153

ISBN 9781922589361

Copyright © Paul Kraus 2023

All rights reserved. Other than for the purposes and subject to the conditions prescribed under the *Copyright Act*, no part of this publication may be reproduced, stored in a retrieval system, or transmitted in any form or by any means, electronic, mechanical, photocopying, recording or otherwise, without the prior permission of the publisher.

Scripture quotations are from the *New Revised Standard Version Bible*, copyright 1989, Division of Christian Education of the National Council of the Churches of Christ in the United States of America. Used by permission. All rights reserved.

One Scripture quotation is from the Holy Bible NEW INTERNATIONAL VERSION®, NIV®, Copyright © 1973, 1978, 1984, 2011 by Biblica, Inc.® Used by permission. All rights reserved worldwide.

Catalogue-in-Publication entry is available from the National Library of Australia
http://catalogue.nla.gov.au

Cover design by Ian James – www.jgd.com.au
Text design by Coventry Press
Set in Fontin

Printed in Australia

**For my wife, Sue...**

Whose selfless love and abundant grace have granted me healing and a certainty in my faith, beyond the staircase of either time or dreams, yet alone my fears. You possess the gentle faith of Mary and perpetually reflect God's love to me. This reality, our unity of love ... will last forevermore.

# Contents

Foreword ................................................. 7
Dedication .............................................. 8

**Faith** ..................................................... 9

    A pilgrimage of faith ............................. 10
    Faith, hope and love – the perfect healers ........... 14
    The four faiths .................................. 15
    The healing power of faith ........................ 18
    Faith and hope – immeasurably victorious .......... 20
    The nature of faith .............................. 23
    A hymn of faith ................................. 24
    Healing is ... ................................... 25
    The shepherd of our soul ......................... 26
    The mystery of Christ ............................ 27
    An abiding prayer ............................... 29
    Inspiring faith and hope .......................... 30

**Hope** .................................................... 31

    The magnificent light of hope ..................... 32
    Peace and hope – a Celtic prayer .................. 33
    A prayer for hope ............................... 34
    The spiritual realm of hope ....................... 35
    Divine encouragement ........................... 37
    Hope ........................................... 38
    New hope, new life .............................. 39
    The gift of healing ............................... 41
    Christ within us – the hope of glory! ............... 43
    In Christ alone my hope is found .................. 44

**Love** .................................................. 46

    The nature of God is love .......................... 47
    Only two loves remain ............................. 49
    The healing power of love ......................... 51
    Let us love one another ........................... 53
    Fear, freedom, love ................................ 54
    An abundance of love .............................. 56
    The love of God ................................... 57
    Jesus' love ........................................ 58
    Mary's song of unending love and praise ........... 60
    A seraphic fire ................................... 62

**Forgiveness and healing** ............................ 64

    Forgiveness, mercy, love .......................... 65
    Forgiveness and love .............................. 66
    The saints can teach us how to forgive ............ 68
    Decide to forgive ................................. 70
    Forgiveness and healing ........................... 72
    The Jesus I never knew ............................ 73

**Listening to God in silence and stillness** .............. 74

    Meditation – a healing form of prayer ............. 75
    Surrender to God in humility and silence .......... 77
    Silence, stillness, solitude ...................... 79
    Meditation and mindfulness: experiencing
    Christ within ..................................... 80
    Meditation and silent prayer ... God is speaking .... 82
    To meditate ....................................... 85

**Living in the power of the Holy Spirit** ............... 86

    To live in the Spirit ............................. 87
    The mystery of silence .......................... 88
    For everything there is a season ................ 89
    A prayer for faith, hope, healing, love .......... 91
    Conversations of the heart ...................... 92
    Harmony, healing, holiness ..................... 93
    Ministry of silence .............................. 95
    Our intimate reality – prayer ................... 97
    The heart of all things .......................... 99
    Heart and voice sing shouts of joy .............. 101
    A holy moment ................................. 103
    A prayer for protection ......................... 104
    Prayer ........................................... 105
    The church's given mission for you ... for me ......... 107
    A prayer for the fullness of healing ............ 108

**Acknowledgements** ................................. 109

# Foreword

In this book, through prayer and prose, Paul Kraus provides glimpses into his experiences of healing. Woven throughout are inspirations from the saints, scripture, and sacred hymnody.

Arguably the central 'healing' theme this book entails is the gentle encouragement to continually relinquish ourselves and our lives into the arms of a loving God. At some point we all reach the end of our resources and some of us cry out to God for healing. In surrender is healing.

While Paul's life story and his experiences of healing are extraordinary, they are also very human and ordinary – hence accessible to us all. Consequently, Paul's book accompanies and invites the reader into a more intentional and compassionate reflection on their own wellsprings of hope. His book also reminds us that we all – whether we are lay or ordained – can craft our own stories into written form as a gift to the Body of Christ.

Paul has graciously gifted this book, with its prayers and prescriptions for healing, to the ministry of Centacare, Brisbane, the social service agency of the Archdiocese of Brisbane. The work of Centacare/Catholic Care is replicated in every Diocese across Australia.

I thank Paul for his generosity and commend his book for your thoughtful reflection.

Paul Jensen<br>
Pastoral Director, Holy Spirit Seminary<br>
Director, Mission and Formation<br>
Centacare, Brisbane

# Dedication

This is a book of prayers and divine promises about the nature of healing. It is written primarily in verse, occasionally in simple poetic form. God's promises come from Biblical verses and from the saints, especially St Augustine, through the pages of Christian history. Also included are hymns whose verses speak to us about God's strength in the realm of how we are healed. It is important to note that curing is not synonymous with healing, which is far more embracing in both time and space. It is possible to be cured, yet not healed.

The following pages deliberately – yet carefully and compassionately – guide one's heart and mind towards a harvest of genuine hope. It does this by initiating a 'voice to the soul,' in a spiritual, rather than an intellectual way.

Faith, hope, love, forgiveness and being aware of God's presence in the sanctity of silence are ways in which the Holy Spirit of God heals people from any kind of difficulty, great or small. The journey of life – unique as it is for every individual – shows that the hand of God comes from surrender, from letting go and letting God.

The prayers and prescriptions for healing in this book are dedicated to the ministry of Centacare, the welfare branch of the Catholic Church based in Brisbane. The work of Centacare is replicated in every Diocese across Australia. However, this book shows us that all of us require healing in one form or another in our lives. Jesus, our risen Lord, helps us, now and forevermore.

# FAITH

## A pilgrimage of faith

I am a child of the Holocaust, born well over three quarters of a century ago in a Nazi forced labour camp in Austria, late in 1944. History stated I should have been born in the greatest death camp of western civilization, Auschwitz. Mother – from Budapest – had been sent there on a cattle train, together with my brother, her two-year old son, in July 1944, when she was pregnant with me.

She had no idea that her husband, our beloved father, had been taken to the infamous concentration camp of Mauthausen, after having worked as a slave labourer, in Slovakia, near Hungary. She travelled in a cattle truck, crammed with people like sheep, with many other unwanted souls. We possessed only God's holy angels and his spirit as we travelled to our imminent death.

In a glorious and completely rare and mysterious way in the history of the Second World War, our lives were saved. Some passengers were off-loaded and taken to a Nazi labour camp in Austria. We were among that group. My mother encountered a prayerful vision on the night of my birth, in October 1944, in a primitive wooden cell in a forced labour camp in beautiful Austria.

In a most vivid fashion, she felt the presence of Jesus on that profound night of her life. Her spiritual revelation uplifted her in body and spirit forevermore. This not merely changed her life, it also permanently altered the future of all of us as well.

Some years after the end of the War our family travelled as Jewish refugees to Australia, at the other end of the earth, far away from my mother's native Budapest. My life has encountered serious illness at various times, yet through God's love and grace, he enabled me to live and to witness his love and freedom so freely.

The purpose of this writing is to illustrate the ways in which complete faith, hope and love shown by the presence of God throughout my life has brought blessing and new life in abundance. Reading his holy word and receiving the presence of Jesus through the truthful and wonderful reality of the sacraments has granted me a living hope, especially when poor medical news virtually overcame my well-being. The emphasis of this writing is to show how simply our faith can be practised.

The powerful meaning and reality of silence and contemplative prayer was a discovery of great value, which these pages joyfully proclaim. It was an important means of 'turning the corner' and slowly recovering, following a diagnosis of serious illness on more than one occasion. Showing the truth of this is the central focus of the following pages.

The following prayers, promises and prescriptions for healing presents a witness to the power of God himself. All of us require some kind of healing in our life, whether physical, emotional or spiritual. My life's motto could easily have been 'survival' in the light of my birth at a time and place when Jewish people were not allowed to live in the darkest days of the Second World War under German occupation. In a glorious – and perhaps miraculous – way, I overcame each life-challenging situation which I encountered in my lengthy life.

God's presence has touched me deeply. Faith, hope, purpose, no less than a sense of the love in which the spirit of Jesus has directly healed me, are aspects of my life that are touched on in this book. My physical healing in the light of serious illness was superimposed by a strong faith and trust in God's mercy and wisdom.

Eternal hope has become an absolute surety of my faith. Jesus' words, 'The kingdom of heaven is within you' has been translated in a variety of highly therapeutic ways, foremost in my spiritual journey.

The theme of this book weaves around the truth of the reality of God's presence and how this can occur throughout our life. There is a harmony in each topic of this book – whether it is the mystery of Jesus, the underlying peace which can permeate the human spirit, or the way holiness is expressed. The notion of prayer and the reality of joy and love in the life of a believer in Jesus, as Lord and Master, gives this book its underlying meaning.

This fact I term as 'necessities of the heart'. We all possess emotions, and our emotional life is frequently tossed around, changed by whatever the circumstance and tide of life might be.

Sadness and joy, peace and suffering, youth, age, as well as the condition of our lifestyle, can significantly impinge on our emotional outlook. Happiness, sadness, contentment or the turbulence of our heart or mind influences our well-being. They can be 'compass points' of our life which form our sense of wellness, or what I call 'wholeness'.

From the Christian – more specifically the Church's – perspective of life, most saints, once termed 'friends of God' have stated that the sacraments are indicators of the mystery of life itself. Baptism, marriage, anointing, reconciliation, silent prayer all provide the spiritual food of life. Above all, in frequently participating in the Eucharist, no less than the blessing of forgiveness and being released into freedom, we also experience the central 'compass point', the spiritual food in our life.

In other words, all of these are Christian mysteries of ethereal beauty, wonder and truth. This final notion is also the key purpose of this book. Its prayers, simple forms of verse, biblical verses, no less than the promising statements by various saints are all designed to make the reader stop and think of the unique priorities of our earthly pilgrimage.

## Faith, hope and love – the perfect healers

Lord, make me an instrument of your peace.
Where there is hatred, let me sow love.
Where there is injury, pardon.
Where there is doubt, faith.
Where there is despair, hope.
Where there is darkness, light.
And where there is sadness, joy.

Divine Master, grant that I may not
Seek to be consoled, as to console,
To be understood, as to understand,
To be loved, as to love.

For it is in giving that we receive.
It is in pardoning that we are pardoned.
It is in dying that we are born to eternal life.

St Francis of Assisi

... Touch me now with your healing hands, for I believe that your purpose for me is to be well in mind, body, soul and spirit. Cover me with the most precious blood of your Son, our Lord Jesus Christ, from the top of my head to the soles of my feet ...

# The four faiths

*(This brief extract explains to followers of Christ, perhaps in a slightly controversial way, the nature of the meaning of the word 'faith'. It places the prayers and promises of these pages into the perspective of our universal need of faith and healing. Its author was not only a paediatric surgeon, but also, eventually, became a best-selling writer on the nature of healing.)*

We have found that four faiths are crucial to recovering from serious illness: faith in oneself, one's doctor, one's treatment, and one's spiritual faith. The last, although seldom totally achievable by most of us, is in many ways a key to the others.

The 'spiritual life' has many meanings. It need not be reflected in any commitment to organised religion, and we all know that some of the most outwardly pious people are the least spiritual. These are the ones who give other people 'spiritual ulcers'.

From the standpoint of a healer, I view spirituality as including the belief in some meaning and order in the universe. I view the force behind creation as a loving, intelligent energy. For some, this is labelled God; for others, it can be seen simply as a source of healing. From this comes the ability to find peace, to resolve the apparent contradictions between one's emotions and reality, between internal and external.

Spirituality means acceptance of what is (not to be confused with resignation or approval of evil). Jesus told us to love our enemies, not like them and not have no enemies.

In an abandoned, bombed-out house in Germany at the end of World War II, Allied soldiers found a testimony to this faith scratched into a basement wall by one of the victims of the Holocaust:

> I believe in the sun – even when it does not shine.
> I believe in love – even when it is not shown.
> I believe in God – even when he does not speak.

Spirituality means the ability to find peace and happiness in an imperfect world, and to feel that one's own personality is imperfect but acceptable. From this peaceful state of mind come both creativity and the ability to love unselfishly, which go hand in hand.

Acceptance, faith, forgiveness, peace and love are the traits that define spirituality for me. These characteristics always appear in those who achieve unexpected healing from serious illness ... A person who believes in a benevolent higher power has a potent reason for hope – and hope is physiologic ...

> Those who profess a faith merely because their parents did or because it increases their social standing are unlikely to really believe it can heal them. Sometimes religion even becomes a negative factor. People think, 'If God gave me this illness, who am I to get well?' ...
>
> I think of God as the same potential healing force – an intelligent, loving energy or light – in each person's life. I suggest that patients think of illness not as God's will but as our deviation from God's will. To me it is the absence of spirituality that leads to difficulties.

The energy of hope and faith is always available. We all must die once, but the spiritual way is always open to everyone and can make our lives beautiful whenever we choose it. As the German dramatist, Christian Friedrich Hebbel once wrote, 'Life is not anything, it is only the opportunity for something.'

Extract taken from *Love, Medicine and Miracles*
by Bernie Siegel, MD
(Used with permission of the publisher,
Arrow Books, London.)

*Faith is to believe what we do not see, and the reward of faith is to see what we believe.*

St Augustine

## The healing power of faith

Why, indeed, does faith heal? Or, perhaps, we might ask how faith heals? There is, at one level at least, no simple answer to such a mysterious and complex question.

A Christian response to why faith heals will take the line that God, through Jesus, loved us so much that he made atonement for our sin on the cross and that all who believe in the Lord Jesus Christ will find forgiveness and healing.

The wonderful thing about God's forgiveness in Christ is that as soon as we sincerely repent of our sins and seek God's forgiveness in Christ, we are released from the power they hold over us. Healing, on the other hand, takes time and is a gradual process of being made whole once again.

In the Gospels, Jesus performed healings on people whose faith and trust in him was strong. For example, Jesus healed the woman who had been suffering from a haemorrhage for twelve years. In faith, she touched the edge of Jesus' cloak, expecting a miracle. In compassion, Jesus turned to her and said, 'Take heart, daughter, your faith has made you well' (Matthew 9:22). Instantly, the woman was healed of her infirmity.

Likewise, in the book of Acts of the Apostles we read of the poor crippled beggar whom Peter healed by faith in the power of the risen Jesus: 'faith in his name... has made this man strong whom you see and know; and the faith which is through Jesus has given the man this perfect health in the presence of you all' (Acts 3:16).

We also know from Scripture that faith in the Son of God is a means by which we can overcome the vicissitudes of life:

'for whatever is born of God conquers the world. And this is the victory that conquers the world, our faith' (1 John 5:4).

Faith and hope go hand in hand. Christians have ample grounds for hope... 'For God so loved the world that he gave his only Son, so that everyone who believes in him may not perish but may have eternal life' (John 3:16).

This is not some 'pie in the sky' hope. Rather, it is a hope based on historical reality through the life and death of Jesus. Our present worries and sufferings pale in comparison to the wonder of God's ultimate promise of a higher hope in this world, wherever it has led us, and the assurance of eternal life.

Who will separate us from the love of Christ? Will affliction or distress or persecution or famine or nakedness or peril or sword? As it is written,

'For your sake we are being killed all day long;
we are accounted as sheep to be slaughtered.'

No, in all these things we are more than victorious through him who loved us. For I am convinced that neither death, nor life, nor angels, nor rulers, nor things present, nor things to come, nor powers, nor height, nor depth, nor anything else in all creation will be able to separate us from the love of God in Christ Jesus our Lord.

(Romans 8:35-39)

## Faith and hope – immeasurably victorious

Hope is a priceless treasure. Promises throughout the Bible, no less than from Jesus himself, inspire hope in us as we read them and are given confidence for the present, no less than the future.

We know that the love and peace of God will eventually prevail, however challenging our circumstance might be. This conditional state of our humanity, especially when expectations and desires we hope for are not realised, can, at times, be devastating.

Yet the Bible goes further in its understanding of the meaning of this word we call 'hope.' It bears a certainty that God's will, however cloudy or vague it might be hidden, will, in God's timing prevail. Our understanding of hope is based upon a wish or desire. The biblical understanding has a firmer ground. In the letter to the Hebrews we read,

> Now faith is the assurance of things hoped for, the conviction of things not seen.
>
> (Hebrews 11:1)

Hope and faith are tied together. In essence, you have hope because you have faith, and you have faith because you have hope. The object of our faith is in the promises of God. These promises are related in many passages throughout Scripture. In every illustration of faith and hope, there is a certain confidence. We must be sure that God will respond in his way for our ultimate good.

Two passages of Scripture illustrate the certainty of hope in God's faithfulness and provision:

> Therefore do not worry, saying, 'What will we eat?' or 'What will we drink?' or 'What will we wear?' For it is the Gentiles who strive for all these things; and indeed your heavenly Father knows that you need all these things. But strive first for the kingdom of God and his righteousness, and all these things will be given to you as well.
>
> (Matthew 6:31-33)

> And my God will fully satisfy every need of yours according to his riches in glory in Christ Jesus.
>
> (Philippians 4:19)

Hope has other highly significant points of clarification and meaning for all of us. The first of these is the hope of God's presence: We read, for example,

> Be strong and bold; have no fear or dread of them, because it is the Lord your God who goes with you; he will not fail you or forsake you. 1 John 5:14-15
>
> (Deuteronomy 31:6)

> And remember, I am with you always, to the end of the age.
>
> (Matthew 28:20)

There are other ways in which the power of hope is so powerful in the life we live. The words of numerous Psalms illustrate how God's love, care and protection are with us.

Above all, we have the solid hope of eternal life in the life and death of Jesus.

We are promised the hope of God's protection, the hope of Christ's return as well as the hope of answered prayer. This hope is illustrated in the following words: ...

> 'And this is the boldness we have in him, that if we ask anything according to his will, he hears us. And if we know that he hears us in whatever we ask, we know that we have obtained the requests made of him'.
>
> (1 John 5:14-15)

What confidence our faith can bring us when we know not only the hope of God's provision – that he will meet all our needs according to the riches of his glory in Christ Jesus (Philippians 4:19) – but we can experience God's presence through both prayer and in the sacrament of holy communion. Further, we can experience the hope, indeed the reality, of God's presence in the benefit of Christian meditation.

> ... but those who wait for the Lord shall renew their strength;
> they shall mount up with wings like eagles;
> they shall run and not be weary;
> they shall walk and not faint.
>
> (Isaiah 40:31)

## The nature of faith

What is faith?

> 'Now faith is the assurance of things hoped for, the conviction of things not seen.'
>
> (Hebrews 11:1)

Faith is so important because it is how we have a relationship with God. We are in God's loving and caring control. It grants each of us a sense of confidence in the here and now.

> 'For by grace you have been saved through faith...'
> (Ephesians 2:8)

Faith is a personal and communal relationship. In the Apostles Creed, we affirm, 'I believe in God'. Our personal faith brings us into a relationship with God and God's people. What hope and wonder does this belief inspire for each of us?

Faith is necessary for salvation: Jesus proclaimed, 'The one who believes and is baptised will be saved' (Mark 16:16). Through faith and being baptised, we belong to the Church and to the family of believers who share eternal life.

Faith is a free, human act, a gift from God which enables us to know and love him. We need to act in faith to respond to the eternal love of Jesus in dying for us on the cross.

Through faith, we have the confidence to know we have a relationship with God. Faith fills us with conviction because of God's promises in his holy word and in the power of the Holy Spirit (1 Thessalonians 1:5).

## A hymn of faith

It is well with my soul.

When peace like a river, attends my way,
When sorrows like sea billows roll
Whatever my lot, you have taught me to say,
It is well, it is well, with my soul.

It is well
With my soul
It is well, it is well with my soul.

While Satan might buffet, though trials should come,
Let this blest assurance control,
That Christ has regarded my helpless estate,
And has shed his own blood for my soul.

It is well, it is well
With my soul, with my soul.
It is well, it is well with my soul.

My sin, oh, the bliss of this glorious thought,
My sin, not in part but the whole,
Is nailed to the cross, and I bear it no more,
Praise the Lord, praise the Lord, O my soul.

It is well, it is well
With my soul, with my soul,
It is well, it is well with my soul.

## Healing is ...

HEALING is filling your mind with God's love and releasing all guilt.

HEALING is turning to God and away from disease and depression.

HEALING is joining your mind and will to God's mind and will.

HEALING is replacing fear with love, anger with peace, guilt with forgiveness.

HEALING is seeing yourself as forgiven and taking delight in it.

HEALING is inner peace which overflows the body.

HEALING is the same as forgiveness.

HEALING is thanking God for what he has already given you.

HEALING is reconciliation between mind and spirit.

HEALING is being humble before God but being powerful in him.

HEALING is freedom from past guilt and anxiety over the future.

(Author unknown, Taken from *Wholeness*,
Anglican Order of St Luke, Melbourne, 1998.)

## The shepherd of our soul

The Lord is my shepherd, I shall never lack anything...
He makes me lie down in green pastures.
He leads me beside still waters, he restores my soul.
He leads me in paths of righteousness for his name's sake.
Even though I walk through the valley of the shadow of death,
I fear no evil.
For you are by my side, your rod and your staff comfort me.
You prepare a table before me in the presence of my enemies.
You anoint my head with oil, and the cup of your goodness overflows.
Surely goodness and mercy shall follow me all the days of my life ...
I shall dwell in the house of the Lord forevermore ...

Amen.

(Psalm 23)

*Understanding is the reward of faith. Therefore, seek not to understand that you may believe, but believe that you may understand.*
St Augustine

## The mystery of Christ

When Jesus appeared on earth, his coming was – for many at that time – without meaning, or even possibly mysterious. St Paul, writing in his letter to the Romans, as well as his letter to the Ephesians, notes this fact. Yet he proclaims that Jesus came ... 'according to the command of the eternal God, to bring about the obedience of faith'. Paul also notes that the mystery of Jesus is 'by revelation... now revealed to his holy apostles and prophets by the Spirit' (see Ephesians 3:5).

Paul emphasised that Jesus was the revelation of God's prophets from earlier times. He acknowledges that Jesus was not only the Messiah of the Jewish people, but to all mankind. Paul also explained that Jesus, the Christ, is the mystery of God (Colossians 2:2.) Jesus, who after his death became the resurrected Christ, is, in a real sense, the mystery of God.

The most wonderful truth is that from the depth of our spiritual experience we can be awakened to the presence of Jesus in our lives, not only in our prayer, but by experiencing the spirit in the breath of Jesus in our lives. We also experience the saintly presence of Jesus in the blessing of receiving holy communion.

Our sense of the sacred through these signposts we experience in our Christian walk through life is a way of finding deep peace. Spiritually, mentally and in an all-embracing way we become truly whole. We will live a life of greater courage, faith and hope, as reflected in the following words of Scripture:

'Be strong and bold; have no fear or dread of them, because it is the Lord your God who goes with you; he will not fail you or forsake you.'

(Deuteronomy 31:6)

Gracious Heavenly Father, grant us the wisdom to discover you,

the intelligence to understand you, the diligence to seek after you,

the patience to wait for you, eyes to behold you, a heart to meditate upon you,

and a life to proclaim you.

Prayer of St Benedict

## An abiding prayer

Supplicating, speaking, beseeching, listening, silence,
prayer, encountering God by widespread means.

Quiet dimension, the Holy Spirit's voice gently shines
in every heart: alive to those who seek God earnestly.

Healing mindfulness for anyone who speaks, raises
or receives the mercy and love of God so fervently.

God reigns for all whose hearts receive his grace,
the glorious from which Jesus in such serenity spoke.

Contemplative prayer, unfathomable love here to share,
Jesus empowers, strengthens, wellness still provokes.

Forgiveness, freedom, redemption, blessed, by a holy fire,
great wealth receives, nominally or powerfully perceived.

Loving devotion fills the heart, in a state, timelessly we feel
tranquility: pure prayer in sinless truth forever lives.

God's power in Jesus grants us faith, love, grace, hope,
touches the spirit with unending Love, endlessly he gives.

## Inspiring faith and hope

Christians have a sure foundation for having hope in their lives. We know that whatever the length of our days, whatever the sufferings we pass through, Jesus, the shepherd of our lives, has trod that path. He has overcome the world and by his death and resurrection we have the assurance of 'overcoming the world' and meeting our Lord face to face.

Hope is inextricably linked to faith and love. A famous nineteenth-century evangelist, Charles Haddon Spurgeon, composed a beautifully concise summary about the connection between faith, hope and love:

> Faith goes up the stairs that love has made and looks out the window that hope has opened.

The eighteenth-century poet and essayist, Oliver Goldsmith, wrote:

> Hope, like the glimmering taper's light,
> Adorns and cheers our way.
> And still, as darker grows night,
> Emits a brighter ray.

There are hundreds of reassuring passages of Scripture about the reason for 'possessing a brighter ray of hope'. Here are two:

> For you, O Lord, are my hope, my trust, O Lord, from my youth. Upon you I have leaned from my birth; it was you who took me from my mother's womb.
>
> (Psalm 71:5-6.)

> May the God of hope fill you with all joy and peace in believing, so that you may abound in hope by the power of the Holy Spirit.
>
> (Romans 15:13.)

# HOPE

## The magnificent light of hope

Faith gives substance to hope. Only faith can make the connection, the leap into the realms of the hoped for, the longed for, and make the way open for God who alone can bring it to pass.

Hope is the bridge over which faith walks hand-in-hand with God. And God who sees the end from the beginning, who calls things that are not as though they were, who speaks the word, and it is so, sees a seed – and by perfect faith calls it a ripened ear of corn, or even a sheath ... or even again, a whole field full, ready for harvest.

Catherine Aldis, *Wholeness*
Order of St Luke, Auckland, New Zealand, 2008

Whatever suffering and sorrow we may go through in this world, a better future awaits us in God. This world is not the end of your story. What awaits us in heaven is a great reward that will make every hardship we're going through worthwhile.

## Peace and hope – a Celtic prayer

The Lord is here,
His Spirit is with us ...

We need not fear,
His Spirit is with us ...

We are surrounded by love,
His Spirit is with us ...

We are immersed in peace,
His Spirit is with us...

We abide in hope,
His Spirit is with us...

We travel in faith,
His Spirit is with us...

We live in eternity,
His Spirit is with us...

The Lord is here,
His Spirit is with us.

David Adam, *The Cry of the Deer*,
Triangle/SPCK 1987.

O Israel, hope in the Lord! For with the Lord there is steadfast love, and with him is great power to redeem...

(Psalm 130:7)

## A prayer for hope

We ask you, God of grace and eternal life, to increase and strengthen the hope within us. Grant us this virtue of being strong, grant us also this power of having confidence in your strength, of possessing a courage that is unshakable. May we always have a desire for your presence. Make us always trust in your faithfulness and hold fast without despondency in the strength of your might.

May we be of this mind and produce this attitude in us by your Holy Spirit. Then, our Lord and God, we shall have the virtue of hope. Then, we can courageously set about the task of our life again and again. Then, we shall be animated by the joyful confidence that we are not working in vain. Then, we shall do our work in the knowledge that is in us, and when our powers fail, you, our Almighty God, according to your good pleasure, are working to your honour and our salvation. Strengthen your hope in us. This, we pray in the name of our Lord Jesus Christ.

Karl Rahner, SJ
*The Need and the Blessing of Prayer*
Liturgical Press, 1997, Minnesota, USA

## The spiritual realm of hope

In the ordinary English vocabulary, *hope* is distinguished from certainty. There is a conditional element attached to its meaning. At times, hope also refers to wishful thinking. It almost bears a religious notion to it, something for which we strongly desire.

Yet, within a biblical realm, the word hope involves distinctly different things – particularly the notions of confidence and trust. This word also conveys anticipation. In his first letter, St Peter wrote 'set all your hope on the grace that Jesus Christ will bring you when he is revealed' (1 Peter 1:13. .Hope, in this context, is not wishful thinking. Rather, it is based on something that will come to pass because God has promised it. set all your hope on the grace that Jesus Christ will bring you when he is revealed.

Hope is a part of our faith. It is an overwhelming reality and a distinct part of our faith. St Paul in Romans writes, 'Faith comes from what is heard and what is heard comes through the word of Christ' (Romans 10:17). Faith and hope are precious promises and, in the life, death and resurrection of Jesus, we may possess God's promise of everlasting life. Hope is invested in and focused on someone, namely the person of Jesus. Hope comes from the promises of God, shown throughout holy scripture, yet they are fulfilled in the life and work of Jesus, our Saviour and risen Lord.

St Paul wrote, 'May the God of hope fill you with all joy and peace' (Romans 15:13). These are hardly words denoting wishful thinking. They grant us sure confidence that both in this life and in the life to come we may know a peace that passes all understanding. Biblical hope is not vain or fanciful thinking. Together with the sacramental signs of divine wonder, especially received in the holy sacrament, we can know the presence of God in our lives. What an enormous difference to what we commonly understand by the word hope.

Christian hope is built on the glorious historical and spiritual reality of what has occurred, namely, what Christ has done for us. He was our Passover Lamb, who died and whose death promised perfect hope, the true reality of everlasting life.

> *When we pray, the voice of the heart must be*
> *heard more than the proceedings from the mouth.*
>
> St Bonaventure

## Divine encouragement

Where can I go from your spirit?

Where can I flee from your presence?

If I go to the heavens, you are there,

If I make my bed in the depths, you are there,

If I rise on the wings of the dawn,

If I settle on the far side of the sea,

Even there your hand will guide me,

Your right hand will hod me fast ...

Even the darkness will not darken you ...

The night will shine like day ...

(Psalm 139, 7-12. NIV Version.)

# Hope

Hope is the thing with feathers -
That preaches in the soul -
And sings the tune without the words -
And never stops at all.

And sweetest in the gale is heard -
And sore must be the storm -
That could abash the little bird -
That kept so many warm.

I've heard it in the chilliest land -
And on the strangest sea -
Yet never in extremity -
It asked a crumb of me.

Emily Dickinson.

Life's ultimate moment of acceptance, hope, life, eternal love ...

This is our hope in Jesus, brother, father, friend, eternal and

risen Lord ...

## New hope, new life

Born into light of survival. Hope or hopeless? Mother's apocalypse. Waiting to outwit them in their dark regime. Antisemitism at its height. Death camps for a thousand years across the Reich prevailed in that distant fateful time. Mother's merest wish: survival to live. To believe in the mercy and compassion of God. To partake of life itself. Love still lived, not sequestered by hopelessness. Born into that evil world. Was life more than mere circumstance? Jesus the Messiah. Profound vision at his birth. Born in an unfortunate time and place. Insecurity, inferiority, inherent in this circumstance. Born to realise that oppression possessed its deepest self.

Born transparent to God's love and care. Messiah's name in earliest years he learnt. Above every other name. Jesus. The Christ. The risen Lord. Beloved Father. Mystery of the Trinity. His ego left aside. He wandered in this selfish world. Born again one future day, thankful to God for precious times. Beautiful wife and children born. Until illness threatened his health, his life.

Born to tread the earth. Both in healing and in health. Born to love his holy word, to feed upon the sacraments. Born forever to thank him for every deed, for life itself now fulfilled. In weakness we are strong, Paul once said. One message from God's holy word. Born to live to thank him eternally. To find healing in Jesus' name. Born to know Christ's suffering atoned forever in our transitory time on earth. Born to enjoy the grace of God, encountered in our living Lord. Born to thank him for everything. One time healed, forever well.

Knowing in heaven we will appear ennobled before our God. Born to thank him for the sanctity of this lengthy pilgrimage. Born to hear God's voice through night and day. Born with unfathomable gratitude that, beyond this life, we meet our Lord. Born to hear angels who will bring us unto Heaven's throne.

'Holy, holy, holy is the Lord God Almighty who was ... and is ... and is to come.'

We must work the works of him who sent me while it is day; night is coming then no one can work.

(John 9:4)

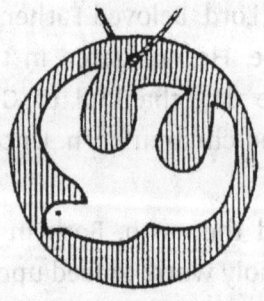

## The gift of healing

Healing the sick in the name of Jesus is one of the most effective tools of evangelisation. Jesus's ministry was primarily as a healer. Healing grants both immediate and far-reaching hope and encouragement to both body and spirit:

> And these signs will accompany those who believe: by using my name they will cast out demons; they will speak new tongues; they will pick up snakes in their hands, and if they drink any deadly thing, it will not hurt them; they will lay their hands on the sick, and they will recover. (Mark 16:17-18)

In the light of what Jesus said, any baptised believer can pray for the sick. The following points are ways of going about the task of healing, wellness and wholeness in body and spirit. They only touch on some aspects of the ministry of healing.

- Relate each day in quietness and in stillness to the Lord. In the words of the Psalmist, 'Be still and know that I am God'. Repeatedly, throughout the word of God, we read of the powerful effects of prayer.
- In deep faith, I prayed for hope with a sense of expectancy. Having been given a poor prognosis after being diagnosed with terminal illness, my faith was, in biblical terms, the size of a mustard seed. Over a length of time, I adopted a highly disciplined lifestyle based on natural healing principles. Despite my 'medical variables', my health eventually stabilised. Slowly, together with a variety of

treatments, I came to realise that the Lord was in control of my life. Whatever lay in the future, with a deep sense of faith, I knew of God's unconditional love for me.
- I was anointed with oil in the name of Jesus, to assist in my healing. (James 5:14, 15)
- I regularly received the blessed Eucharist. Each time I knew the strength and presence of Jesus' love.

## Christ within us – the hope of glory!

Many verses throughout Scripture tell us we are made in the likeness of God's and that he dwells within each one of us. This is a strong reason for possessing an expectant, confident faith, whatever form of healing we – or our loved ones – may require.

These verses from Scripture, together with the blessings the Church freely bestows on us represent powerful ways of being in 'a hope of glory'. The reality of being anointed, receiving the sacrament of the Eucharist, and humbly being reconciled to God's mercy, love and compassion represent powerful ways of being in 'a hope of Glory', not merely in some kind of abstract or ethereal way, but in the reality of our day-to-day life.

The following biblical verses remind us that our lives are incomplete when we forget or ignore the power of the transcendent God who dwells within each heart.

> Do you not know that your body is a temple of the Holy Spirit, who is within you, which you have from God? (1 Corinthians 6:19)

> Let the peace of Christ rule in your hearts, to which indeed you were called in one body. And be thankful. Let the word of Christ dwell in you richly; teach and admonish one another in all wisdom, and with gratitude in your hearts sing psalms, hymns, and spiritual songs to God. (Colossians 3:15,16)

> No-one has ever seen God; if we love one another. God abides in us, and his love is perfected in us ... God is love, and those who abide in love abide in God, and God abides in them. (1 John 4:12,16)

## In Christ alone my hope is found

(What timeless hope, what endless wonder, what great love, what firmer faith is found in the words of the following hymn! What an incredibly powerful prayer of hope and love this hymn expresses.)

In Christ alone my hope is found
He is my light, my strength, my song.
This cornerstone, this solid ground
Firm through the fiercest drought and storm.
What heights of love, what depths of peace
When tears are stilled, when strivings cease,
My comforter, my all in all.
Here in the love of Christ I stand.

In Christ alone who took on flesh
Fullness of God in helpless babe.
This gift of love and righteousness
Scorned by the ones he came to save.
Till on the Cross as Jesus died,
The wrath of God was satisfied,
For every sin on him was laid:
Here in the death of Christ I live.

There in the ground his body lay,
Light of the world by darkness slain.
Then bursting forth in glorious day,
Up from the grave he rose again.
And as he stands in victory,
Sin's curse has lost its grip on me:

For I am his and he is mine,
Bought with the precious blood of Christ.

No guilt in life, no fear in death,
This is the power of Christ in me.
From life's first cry to final breath
Jesus commands my destiny.
No power of hell, nor scheme of man
Can ever pluck me from his hand
'Til he returns or calls me home
Here in the power of Christ I'll stand.

Stuart Townend

# LOVE

## The nature of God is love

Despite all that has been written about the characteristics of God, especially throughout the pages of Scripture, essentially God is one whose love is pervasive. His nature is that God is a God of love and hope. It is equally true that life and holiness also present our understanding of God's nature.

Love is the very essence of who God is, despite the happiness, sadness, mysterious tragedy of our human condition. In the first letter of John, we read: so we know and believe the love God has for us. God is love, and those who abides in love abide in God (1 John 4:16). In other words, love is the greatest and purest essence of who a person is and its proper expression and fulfilment.

However, God's love is not like the love expressed by many in our culture today, which is a love of convenience and ego. To-day's love is at times conditional, something which is virtually 'earned', so to speak. God's love is unconditional. It is one which never fails. As expressed by the Psalmist '... I trust in the steadfast love of God forever and ever' (Psalm 52:8).

For those who belong to Christ, love is the very essence of our life, in its fullness and in its transformation. God's love is not an abstract ideal. Rather, it is a concrete reality which fulfils our emotional and spiritual needs. God's love, compassion and mercy are the very purpose of Christ's giving of himself in the Eucharist. Here we find forgiveness and a healing which is all-encompassing. We receive the Passover Lamb of Jesus in Holy Communion. His love is everlasting, just as we are embraced by eternal peace and joy when we reach God's heavenly kingdom.

What an overwhelming reality of love this act of the sacrifice of God, through Jesus, is to all who, in an unconditional way, as we receive the body and blood of Jesus; and our mortality rests in immortality.

Above all, clothe yourselves with love, which binds everything together in perfect harmony. And let the peace of Christ rule in your hearts, to which indeed you were called ... and be thankful. (Colossians 3:14, 15)

## Only two loves remain

There are two loves only, Lord,
Love of myself and love of you and others.
Each time that I love myself, it's a little less love for you ...
And for others.
It's a draining away of love, it's a loss of love,
For love is made to leave self and fly toward others,
Each time it is diverted towards me, it withers, rots, dies.
Love of self, Lord, is a poison that I absorb each day.
Love of self chooses the best part and keeps the best place.
Love of self indulges my senses and supplies them from others' needs.
Love of self speaks about myself; deafens me from others' words.
Love of self chooses and forces that choice on a friend.
Love of self puts on a false front. It wants me to shine,
Overshadowing other.
Love of self is self-pitying and overlooks the suffering of others.
Love of self thinks me virtuous; it calls me a good man.
Love of self induces me to earn money, to spend it for my pleasure,
To save it for my future.
Love of self advises me to give to the poor, to ease my conscious,
To live in peace.
Love of self is a stolen love,
It was destined for others, they needed it to live, to thrive, and I have diverted it.

So, the love of self creates human suffering.
Help me to love, Lord,
Not to waste my powers of love,
To love myself less and less, to love others more,
And more, and even more,
That around me, no-one should suffer or die –
because I have stolen the love they needed to live.

Michel Quoist, Prayers of Life<br />Gill & Macmillan, Dublin, 1969

*Our hearts were made for you, O Lord, and*
*outwardly they are restless until they rest in you.*
St Augustine, The Confessions

## The healing power of love

In a very real sense, love, kindness and compassion heal. This might sound commonplace, maybe even a trite phrase, yet it contains more than a seed of truthfulness. Love is the most powerful of our emotions. Love is of the mind, not the body. It treads where the intellect is unable to walk. In all kinds of ways, love does enhance the healing process.

'Healing' refers to attaining peace of mind, having freedom from fear, anxiety and experiencing unconditional love. The word 'healing' is not synonymous with 'cure'. Healing is certainly not restricted to a physical cure, which might, or might not, eventuate.

Love and healing are always possible, irrespective of a cure taking place. On this side of the grave, we can never hope to understand the mystery of why some people recover, while others do not.

The road to healing has many different paths, according to our personality type, or our philosophy of life, but love is a fundamental attribute which transcends these variables. Love, like faith, means different things to different people, but whatever its meaning, for an individual, most would agree that love has a spiritual dimension. The Jews believe in the love of the great God of Abraham, Isaac and Jacob and Christians also believe this, as well as the love of Jesus, the Lord Incarnate, whose humanity was lived for the redemption of humankind.

Perhaps the most potent way that love heals is that it helps to release our fear and guilt over our innate tendency not to forgive our wrong doings. Fear and bitterness block a person's ability to heal, whereas love helps the body and mind to heal itself.

The healed mind has a unity about it which contains God's merciful and loving thoughts. Healing possesses harmony of body and spirit. Love expresses a completeness, and a unity, whether or not physical healing occurs.

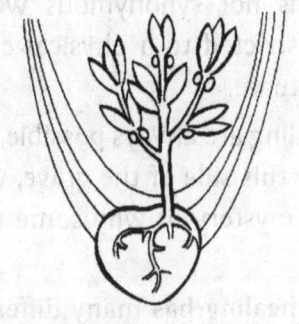

## Let us love one another

Beloved, let us love one another; for love is from God; everyone who loves is born of God and knows God. Whoever does not love does not know God; for God is love. God's love was revealed among us in this way: God sent his only Son into the world, so that we might live thought him.

In this is love, not that we loved God but that he loved us and sent his Son to be the atoning sacrifice for our sins.

God is love, and those who abide in love abide in God, and God abides in them ...

There is no fear in love, but perfect love casts out fear ...

1 John 4:7,8,9.10,16,18.

Love him totally who gave himself totally for your love.

## Fear, freedom, love

Fear imprisons. Love liberates.
Fear paralyses. Love empowers.
Fear disheartens. Love encourages.
Fear sickens. Love heals.
Fear makes us useless. Love makes us productive.
We tune into that perfect love in prayer

...The first step that God takes towards us is that of a love that anticipates and is unconditional. God is the first to love. God does not love because there is something in us that engenders love. God loves us because he himself is love, and, by its very nature, love tends to spread and give itself. God does not even condition his benevolence on our conversion. If anything, this is a consequence of God's love. Saint Paul expresses this perfectly: 'God proves his love for us in that while we still were sinners Christ died for us' (Romans 5:8).

While we still were sinners ... an unconditional love. We were 'distant', as was the prodigal son in the parable: 'while he was still far off, his father saw him and was filled with compassion...' (Luke 15:20).

We are God's beloved children. But is it possible that God has some children whom he does not love? No. We are all God's beloved children ...

The truth of everything is that relationship of love which links the Father to the Son through the Holy Spirit, a relationship into which we are welcomed, thanks to grace. In him, in Jesus Christ, we were all wanted, loved, desired. There is Someone who has impressed within us a primordial beauty, which no sin, no bad choice can ever completely erase. In the eyes of God, we are always small fountains made to gush forth good water. Jesus says to the Samaritan woman: 'the water that I will give... will become... a spring of water gushing up to eternal life' (John 4:14) ...

A wind of liberation blows fear and unhappiness from our faces ... the gift of hope, from God's love is sprouting. And the hope is that of God the Father who loves us as we are: he loves us all, now and forevermore.

*God's Love Is Unconditional*, Pope Francis.

Taken from *L'Osservatore Romano*

16 June 2017, p. 3

There is no fear in love, but perfect love casts out fear; for fear has to do with punishment, and whoever fears has not reached perfection in love.

1 John 4:18

## An abundance of love

If I can stop one heart from breaking,
I shall not live in vain,
If I can ease one life the aching,
Or cool one pain,
Or help one fainting robin
Unto his nest again,
I shall not live in vain.

Emily Dickinson

For God so loved the world that he gave his only Son, so that everyone who believes in him may not perish but may have eternal life.

John 3:16

## The love of God

God's eternal love encircles, embraces
heart and soul, leaves aside all thought,
believes, seeks Christ's sacrifice, forgives
sin eternally by his everlasting Cross.

Sacred sacraments surround, immerses a prayer,
imbues life with faith sublime, yet tender humble,
glorious love beseeches, knows, invites the Spirit
of the Lord, anoints each tender heart.

Eternal prayer surpassing time, embracing hope
beyond the brevity of life, the love of Jesus
spoke in gospel stories told to rich, to poor
throughout the world, whatever time.

The Incarnation, covenant divine, response,
yet mystery, through the Holy Spirit
deeply felt in every age: from Jesus' presence.
Holy Spirit gently receives, now inherits.

Great truth within each heart, mind, spirit,
forever touches our inner being.
God's love in Jesus upon me now
in wonder, freed from bondage forevermore.

The Spirit of the Lord is on me now, poured
Like oil to bless the self, both heart and mind.
Saints of every age adored and loved,
God's everlasting gift forever found.

## Jesus' love

We believe that where people come together
in love ... God is present ...
and good things happen ...
and life is full ...

We believe that we are immersed in mystery ...
That our lives are more than they seem ...
That we belong to each other ...
And to a universe of great creative energies
Whose source and destiny is God.

We believe that God is after us ...
That he is calling us from the depth
Of human life.

We believe that God has risked himself
And become man in Jesus ...
And with Jesus we believe that each of us
Is situated in the love of God ...
And the pattern of our life will be
The pattern of Jesus ...
Through death to resurrection.

And most deeply we believe
That in our struggle to love
We incarnate God in the world.
And so ... aware of mystery and wonder,
Caught in friendship and laughter,
We become speechless before joy fills
Our hearts as we celebrate the sanctity

Of life in the wonder, the strength, power, glory, redeeming love of the blessed Eucharist.

## Mary's song of unending love and praise

Mary greatly rejoices, unified in holiness, joy, mercy, tenderness, praise. Song of hope sung from her Jewish faith, exalting God and her ancestors, recited to witness an obedience to God's loving grace. *My soul magnifies the Lord,* sacred canticle of Marcy commences. Sublime poetic manifestation intones the Virgin's praise. *And my spirit rejoices in God my Savior*: sheer uniform harmony here. *He has regarded the lowliness of his handmaiden.* Mary's voice, in total faith, manifestly innocent, lived – in complete humility. Mother of Jesus in heaven ordained. *All generations shall call me blessed. He who is mighty has done great things for me, and holy is his name.* Gabriel's signature, sign of Mary's inner wealth. *And his mercy is from generation to generation on those who fear him.* Her obedience, an archetype of perfect trust. *He has shown might with his arm, He has scattered the proud in the conceit of their heart and has exalted the lowly* ... courageous, without fear, yet believing Joseph's strength and love. Shielded by humility and lowliness. Jesus, her baby born to bring light to the Gentiles ... glory to his people Israel, Simeon prophesied. Mary, in weakness shown. Powerful love glorified her holiness. *He has filled the hungry with good things and the rich he has sent empty away.*

The Messiah, ever faithful, ever true to one, to all, both rich and poor. *He has given help to Israel, his servant, mindful of his mercy, even as he spoke to our ancestors, to Abraham and to his posterity forevermore.* Mary's majestic gratitude. Her heart, her adoration now revealed.

The Divine Child in her womb she bore in perfect humility and love, obedience, hope ... Mary's praise in this resplendent prayer, soulfully sung by priests and prophets in every age. Let Mary's soul be shared in us: to glorify the risen Lord.

Mary's spirit mirrors discipline, gratitude, obedience and love. We rejoice in this liturgical song of our faith, now and forevermore.

And Mary said,
'My soul magnifies the Lord...'

Luke 1:46

Steadfast love and faithfulness will meet;
righteousness and peace will kiss each other.
Faithfulness will spring from the ground,
and righteousness will look down from the sky.

Psalm 85:10-11

## A seraphic fire

His world aflame, in mid-life serious
illness discovered. Terminal, they thought.
Fiery flames burnt within, without.
Confusion, fear, uncertainty at first
Blackened his impoverished mind.

Accidental diagnosis bewildered him,
Anguish in mysterious ways arrived.
Stumbling confounded his fragile mind.
Spiritual decay briefly metastasised.
The Holy Spirit's power imbued
Stillness, restored a healing
Path from this cancerous way.

Soothing healing ambience soon embraced,
Through meditation and contemplative prayer,
A gift and precious sacrament, unimpeded
Protection from these worldly ills.
Like Mary, mother of hope, who knew
God's love, grace by obedience
to his holy power and word.
Love and faith forever held supreme.

Redemption, whatever circuitous
Paths God had called through infinite
Faith, not fortuitous, yet truly planned.
Whatever news arrived in those distant
Days and times: anointed, blessed, prayed,
Believing God's love forever held ...
Transcendent in its very being.

A pure seraphic fire kindled, healed,
By flames destroying this world's ills.
All will one day be well ... be well.
A disciplined life brought wholeness,
empowerment, a new reality dwells
Within instilling faith and hope,
Wellness in this sanctity of love.

# FORGIVENESS AND HEALING

If we confess our sins, he who is faithful and just will forgive us our sins and cleanse us from all unrighteousness. If we say we have not sinned, we make him a liar, and his word is not in us.

1 John 1: 9-10

God's forgiveness is what we all need, and it is the greatest sign of his mercy. A gift that every forgiven sinner is called upon to share with every brother and sister he or she meets.

Pope Francis, General Audience, 30 March 2016

## Forgiveness, mercy, love

Bless the Lord, O my soul,
And forget not all his benefits.

He pardons all iniquities,
He heals all your ills.

He redeems your life from destruction,
He crowns you with kindness and compassion ...

The Lord works vindication and justice,
For all who are oppressed ...

The Lord is merciful and gracious,
Slow to anger and abounding in steadfast love ...

For as the heavens are high above the earth,
So great is his steadfast love toward those who fear him...

*Extracts from Psalm 103*

## Forgiveness and love

Most Christians, irrespective of their theological differences, would state that God is love and that forgiveness is a manifestation of love. God's character and essence is love. His every intention for his creatures is their highest welfare.

Even before the time of creation, God knew that Adam would sin. At that time of our first creation, God had designed a way for sins to be forgiven. Even in the earliest books of the Bible, in Genesis, Exodus, Deuteronomy, and so on, the notion of forgiveness of sins was described. Certainly, in the death of Christ through the atoning sacrifice of Jesus, we are left in no doubt that God's love ensured the forgiveness of our sins.

The manifestation of forgiveness was fully revealed in the Incarnation of Jesus into our history. By the fact that we were created into the image of God, we are also to love. Even though sinners, we must develop a character that is ready to forgive.

We read, 'Beloved, let us love one another, because love is from God; everyone who loves is born of God and knows God. Whoever does not love does not know God, for God is love' (1 John 4:7, 8).

The apostle Peter once asked Jesus how often he should forgive others (Matthew 18:21). Peter suggested seven times. But Jesus responded, 'seventy times seven'. Jesus showed how we need to put love into practice.

In the eyes of God, forgiveness is a very serious matter. If we are incapable or unwilling to forgive others, then God might not forgive the sins we continually perform. We need to stop, be mindful and to acknowledge that we also have our weaknesses which need forgiveness.

Writing to the Corinthians, St Paul describes love in action:

> 'Love is patient; love is kind; love is not envious or boastful or arrogant or rude It does not insist on its own way; it is not irritable or resentful; it does not rejoice in wrongdoing, but rejoices in the truth. It bears all things, believes all things, hopes all things, endures all things.
>
> 1 Corinthians 13:4-7

If we loved like this, we would not be offended or so often hurt. We would not even notice the slights or minor arguments and disagreements we inevitably face. If we followed what St Paul writes, there would be nothing to forgive because 'love covers a multitude of sins' (1 Peter 4:8).

The grace and love of the promises of the Bible – yet yet alone the sacrament of reconciliation – is vital to each of us to find, as we seek love and forgiveness. The Passover of the Lamb, which we term the Eucharist initiated by Jesus to his followers, allows us to perceive the ways in which forgiveness and love are integral to the normal, emotional necessities of our hearts and our lives.

## The saints can teach us how to forgive

Because of our human nature, all of us tend to live with an 'inbuilt' vengeance. We easily forget what St Paul wrote about the nature of vengeance, which we sometimes throw into the 'too hard' basket:

> 'Bless those who persecute you; bless and do not curse them... Do not repay anyone one evil for evil but take thought for what is noble in the sight of all ... live peaceably with all... vengeance is mine, I will repay, says the Lord. No, if your enemies are hungry, feed them; if they are thirsty, give them something to drink; for by doing this you will heap burning coals on their heads. Do not be overcome by evil but overcome evil with good.'
>
> Romans 12:14, 17, 18, 19, 20, 21

The first Christian martyr, St Stephen, gives us a powerful example of Christian forgiveness. The Acts of the Apostles tells us how he was stoned for his fearless proclamation of the gospel. His last words were, 'Lord, do not hold this sin against them' (Acts 7:60).

Our Lord's parable of the unforgiving servant (Matthew 18:23-25) reminds us that if we insist on strict justice in the cases of those who have sinned against us, we will also be held liable for our own offenses against God. The lives of the saints showed their humility and honesty in all aspects of their lives, including their sinfulness. St Augustine is a prime example of this in his writing of the Confessions. One illustration of this is his remark,

There are many kinds of alms, the giving of which helps us to obtain pardon for our sins; but none is greater than that by which we forgive from our own heart a sin someone has committed against us.

In God's eyes, the most dignified response to an injury is to turn the other cheek. Sometimes forgiving those who wrong us can set the stage for miracles of grace and lovingkindness. Forgiving others can indeed be difficult, mainly because anger and resentment, no less than a natural desire for revenge, virtually demands fervent and honest prayer. All the saints showed and taught that we need to forgive our enemies, for Christ will reign only in a heart that seeks to be at peace.

> *Where there is no love, pour love in, and you will draw love out.*
>
> St John of the Cross

## Decide to forgive

So that we can allow healing, in its fullest sense, to occur – physical and emotional or spiritual – it is important that we try to release the poisonous effects of negative emotions, such as bitterness, resentment and guilt, by forgiving. This, at times, might require determination and —especially if our hurt is considerable – strength. When we are unable to forgive, we impede the ability of healing to take place. The following verses illustrate the importance of the act of forgiveness.

> For resentment is negative,
> Resentment is poisonous.
> Resentment diminishes,
> Devours the self.
>
> Be the first to forgive,
> To smile and take the first step:
> You will see happiness bloom
> On the face of your human
> Brother or sister.
>
> Be always the first,
> Do not wait for others to forgive,
> For by forgiving
> You become the master of fate,
> The fashioner of life,
> The doer of miracles.
>
> To forgive is the highest,
> Most beautiful form of love.
> In return you will receive
> Untold peace and freedom.

Dr Robert Muller<br>Assistant Secretary, United Nations

## Forgiveness and healing

If you forgive others their trespasses, your heavenly Father will also forgive you; but if you do not forgive others, neither will your Father forgive your trespasses.

(Matthew 6:14-15)

*Forgiveness is a final form of love.*
Rienhold Niehbuhr Pastor, Theologian

## Forgiveness and healing

When Jesus teaches us to forgive one another, the act of pardoning is not about power, but about conversion. Forgiveness is about letting go of the resentment or anger or hurt that is poisoning our soul. It is a gift we give another who has wronged us, but it is also a gift to ourselves. Forgiveness doesn't always come easily - we sometimes can't help but cling to a sense of righteousness - but not being able to forgive leads to a hard heart that holds us back from seeking the good and living our lives fully. A hardness that Jesus counsels us to reject. The habitual practice of forgiveness brings the kingdom of God closer. It can change us. It can change our world. Let each of us pray that we may be granted hearts to find healing and surrender in our soul.

## The Jesus I never knew

God's silent language, half a life it took to understand,
translate, yet Jesus prayed, his stories tell.
Heartfelt presence, glorious immanence, total awareness.

Listening to Jesus silently, apostles, believers, disciples
who pray in a contemplative way: God's eternal presence
found in silent prayer, since earliest Christian times.

Selfishness from a distance trails, forgiveness found,
redeemed in a joy only the power of Jesus can inspire.
Peace reigns, his love heals, the spirit healed, fulfilled.

Mindful thoughts disappear, silently repeat a sacred
word, invokes silence, peacefulness.
'My heart is restless until it rests in you,' a joy created.

Silence, stillness, forgiveness, this prayer by Jesus
through Mary's not Martha's compassion.
A gentleness wrought by gentleness and love.

Patience, faith, hope leads into spiritual quiet,
hope and love through our eternal Lord.
Acceptance by grace forever found.

Passover Lamb, Jewish roots of the Eucharist.
The Last Supper, from ancient Jewish eyes.
Jesus, atoning, sacrificial Lamb, our holy synthesis.

# LISTENING TO GOD IN SILENCE AND STILLNESS

'What we need most in order to make progress is to be silent before this great God with our appetite and with our tongue, for the language he best hears is silent love.'

St John of the Cross

'Contemplative prayer is nothing else but a secret, peaceful, and loving infusion of God, which, if admitted, will set the soul on fire with the Spirit of love.'

St John of the Cross

'We need stillness and silence to be able to touch souls ... to be able to hear ourselves ... God is the friend of silence.'

Mother Teresa

## Meditation – a healing form of prayer

The following is a piece of verse I wrote many years ago, when I was seriously ill, after I was informed to 'enjoy the rest of my days' because 'medicine could help me no further'. Meditation, contemplative prayer, 'letting go of myself' and, in silence and stillness, allowing God's presence to become present within me, was then unknown to me. It was through the influence of an elderly friend that I became acquainted with an altogether different form of prayer than spoken prayer to which, throughout my life, I had been accustomed. One of the blessings of that illness was that I came to know God's presence in an altogether different and far more intimate way. The following verse I wrote while I was still recovering from serious illness, so many years ago. In an authentic way, I learnt the reality of what Jesus meant when he said, 'The Kingdom of Heaven is within you'.

> Warning bells
> ring false alarms
> to ignorant minds,
> as once they did
> in mine.
>
> Fickle winds
> of prejudice
> blew meditation
> beyond my reach.
>
> Until one day circumstance
> cruelly intervened.
> 'Cancer is a word,

not a sentence,'
they told me ...

That fearful word
which held me in its
vice-like grip.

Softly and gently
meditation beckoned,
gently called:
'Try my healing power',
it quietly said.

My mind wavered
like a summer breeze.
Imperceptibly,
meditation massaged
my fear away.

Knowledge ... no,
a state of mind,
simply, effortlessly
gained, gently ...
gradually showed
meditation enhancing
the healing power,
of spoken prayer.

## Surrender to God in humility and silence

St Augustine lived in the early Christian era, born about AD 354. Although only partially from a Christian background, he was brought up as a Christian in the north African city of Carthage. He lived a tumultuous life, yet finally he became the Bishop of Hippo. He lived in the community of his cathedral clergy.

He wrote many books including The Confessions and The City of God. His writings have made a powerful mark on Christian history. They focus on renouncing the lifestyle of this world and living life to its fullest. The following is a summary taken from The Confessions, focusing on meditation and contemplative prayer.

For St Augustine, God is at the centre of our being and so he invites us to return to ourselves – to come back from our wandering 'out there'. He tells God as revealed in his The Confessions, 'I looked for you everywhere, and you were within me all the time'.

In Augustine's terms, we return to the heart by being still, in body, mind and spirit. 'God speaks to us in the great silence of the heart', he wrote.

Contemplation and meditation are closely related and involve finding similar ways of finding the presence of God within. Meditation achieves this by constantly repeating a sacred word to invoke a quiet mind, and ultimate silence from noises that constantly disturb our mind and take us from God's presence. Contemplation is the simple awareness and focus of the presence of God. It is a realisation that our Lord dwells within our hearts.

We move into a state of contemplative prayer and meditation in a very simple way by sitting still in a peaceful and quiet setting and letting go of the chatter of our minds, no less than the turmoil of our emotions, to a place into a state of silence. The actual method used to practice Christian meditation is outlined in the next section. St Augustine, an early Christian saint, very briefly summarised what Christian meditation attempts to show us by these words:

> *Let us leave a little room for reflection in our lives, room too for silence. Let us look within ourselves and see whether there is some delightful hidden place inside where we can be free of noise and argument. Let us hear God's word in stillness and perhaps we will then come to understand it. Meditation is finding the peace of God within.*
>
> St Augustine *Sermon 52, 22*

## Silence, stillness, solitude

A mysterious part of us, perhaps our DNA, yearns silence,
as intuitively we search, we seek calmness, peace, clarity.

Stillness, silence seem foreign, unrelenting palpable sounds
constantly intrude as quietness fails to find its true reality.

Contemplation and meditation, at once aware of God's presence,
releases heart and mind, listens in awareness, with no duality.

Silence reveals genuine faith, unending hope when harmony,
wholeness, peace prevails, finding here the spirit's true reality.

Seeds now harvest, grow, burgeon, flower, one day in fullness
find as the Spirit moves, miraculously changing our necessity.

In silence, in God's immanence we stand, strife receding,
the selfless soul in faith as material matters disappear.

Holiness gained by silently repeating our mantra or sacred word,
inducing a state, just simply being, as the Holy Spirit intercedes.

Prayer of the heart, silence of the soul, historically heard,
seen by numerous saints and sinners' inner peace.

Timelessly moments stand and flow, peaceful river flows
unceasingly. Silently, God's presence will never cease.

## Meditation and mindfulness: experiencing Christ within

Being still in body, mind and spirit, the practice of meditation, is common to the experience of many religions worldwide. Yet it may also be a special way of finding the spirit of Jesus within our hearts and minds. We call this experience Christian mindfulness.

It is a non-judgmental awareness of experience as it unfolds, moment by moment. In Christian terminology, it is based on the verse 'Be still and know that I am God' (Psalm 46:10). Many other biblical references speak about the silence of God within.

Meditation and a state of mindfulness involve making space to hear God's voice in our hearts. It also involves letting go of our emotions, impulses and needs and moving into a more intimate relationship with God, where we learn to 'pray without ceasing'. We cease the noises that constantly revolve in our lives and move into the practice of contemplative prayer. Meditation implies deepening one's Christian faith, opening the heart to an intimacy with God. Mother Teresa, who became St Mother Teresa, the founder of the Sisters of Charity in India, expressed both Christian meditation and mindfulness in a very beautiful way in the following words:

> 'We need to find God and he cannot be found in noise and restlessness. God is the friend of silence. See how nature – trees, flowers, grass – grows in silence; see the stars, the moon, and the sun, how they move in silence

'... the more we receive in silent prayer, the more we can give in our active life. We need to be silent to touch souls. God speaks to us and through us. All our words will be useless unless they come from within – words which do not give the light of Christ to increase in our darkness.'

*In silence, God ceases to be an object and becomes an experience.*

Thomas Merton

## Meditation and silent prayer ... God is speaking

Allowing God's presence to enter our self, into our heart and spirit in silence, within a specifically Christian context, historically has been done in numerous ways.

Some Christians frown upon the idea of meditation, believing it to be unscriptural and a practice that borders on something pagan. Yet this practice does not merely entail emptying the mind. Rather it is based on stilling the mind and realising the presence and the spirit of God within. Jesus stated that 'the kingdom of heaven is within you'. The Psalmist, at a much earlier time, had stated, 'Be still, and know that I am God'. There are many biblical references to silence and stillness inducing a sense of sanctity. Meditation, as a form of prayer, is about becoming more aware of the presence of God in our life.

### Entering the silence

John Main, a Benedictine monk, introduced Christian Meditation into the Benedictine Monastery in London in 1975. Sometime later, he also introduced this practice to Canada. Gradually, Christian Meditation groups spread world-wide, including Australia.

One of his many comments about what practising meditation means is: 'Meditation is a simple means of leading us into an integral awareness of the nature of our own being ... that we belong to God'. On many occasions, he stated that the emotional noise combines with the turbulent nature of our minds.

Here a few simple guidelines for moving into 'sacred silence.'

### (1) *Phase of relaxation*

Sit down, maintaining a comfortable, but not too comfortable posture, making sure that you relax the body, but at the same time keeping inwardly alert. The practice of meditation involves being aware of our silence in a contemplative way. Now take a few 'letting go' breaths, paying attention to your breathing.

Breathe out tension and worry and feel this occurring. Preferably with your eyes closed (although this is not necessary), visualise any tension melt away.

Let your mind, heart, will and feelings become tranquil and serene. It might be that you spend most of this time in this phase. There are no 'rules' to meditating. This is a time of achieving peace, harmony and unity and allowing the grace and love of God to pour into our hearts. Whatever circumstance arises, surrender yourself, let go of yourself, your mind, your ego, to God himself.

### (2) *Phase of awareness of God's presence*

In the stillness, be assured that God knows you better than you know yourself. God is the one in whom we live and move and have our being. Through Jesus we call God 'Abba', Father. In this phase, our hearts come to God in full confidence that he is with us now. We surrender our wills to God's will so that Christ can reign in our hearts. We accept Jesus as Sovereign

Lord and put ourselves in his control. We put self aside self and enthrone Jesus in our hearts.

### (3) *Phase of forgiveness*

If we have a sense of guilt, shame or fear, if we have a sense of unworthiness before God, our heavenly Father, we need to remove that barrier. One writer has said that it is a healing grace to surrender our sinfulness to his mercy.

### (4) *Phase of contemplation*

With pure hearts, in response to God's love, we can 'rest in stillness, in silence into the presence of the Lord'. We can do this by means of repeating a biblical phrase, already suggested, or by listening to our breath as a means of moving into prayerful silence, or by repeating a sacred word. Simply relax and release everything into God's presence within.

This is the spiritual reality within which we have our being: sharing in the very being of God and offering thanks for his loving presence.

John Main, OSB

## To meditate

We need to surrender ourselves, our ego, our self ...
We need to submit to the truth of who and how we are ...
We need to release our minds to Scripture's eternal truth ...
We need to allow false images to flow from us ...
We need to be aware that silence finds our true reality.
We need to allow the Spirit of Jesus to dwell within ...
We need to respect and love ourselves for who we really are ...
We need to distil the falsities inherent in this life ...
We need to travel within and beyond our minute selves ...
We need to realise this great gift, our unity to be sublime ...
We need to acquire a prayerful faith to find our Lord ...
We need discipline to daily practise this listening form of prayer ...
We need this quiet pilgrimage to journey through life's transient land ...
We need abundant thanks to Jesus, our Christ, our risen Lord ...
We need gratitude for God's Power, everlasting hope, eternal love.

# LIVING IN THE POWER OF THE HOLY SPIRIT

The Holy Spirit you have planted in my heart ... Thank you, God, ... For your life sustaining signs and sacraments ... Thank you, God ... For heart, mind, spirit ... endless thanks be given ... For having created me to love you for eternity ... Thank you my living Lord ... my Jesus ... Christ ... everlasting God ...

For it was you who formed my inward parts; you knit me together In my mother's womb.
I praise you, for I am fearfully and wonderfully made.

Psalm 139:13-14

It is that very Spirit bearing witness with our spirit that we are children of God, and if children, then heirs, heirs of God and joint heirs with Christ - if in fact we suffer with him so that we may also be glorified with him.

Romans 8:16

Be still, and know that I am God ...

Psalm 46:10

## To live in the Spirit

To live in the Spirit of God is to be a listener.
It is to keep the vigil of mystery,
earth less still.
One leans to catch the stirring of the Spirit.
Strange as the wind's will.

The soul that walks where the wind of the Spirit blows
Turns like a wandering weathervane towards love.
It may lament like Job or Jeremiah,
Echo the wounded heart, the single dove.
It may rejoice in spaciousness of meadow,
That emulates the freedom of the sky.

Always it walks in a listless way.
It has cast down forever from its hand
The compass of the whither and the why.

To live with the Spirit of God is to be a lover.
It is becoming love, and like to him
Towards whom we strain with metaphors of creatures:
Fore-sweep and water-rush and the world's whom.
The soul is all activity, all silence.
And though it surges Godward to its goal,
It holds as moving earth holds sweeping noonday,
peacefulness that is the listening of the soul.

Jessica Powers, 1905-1988
Poet, Writer, Carmelite nun, Christian mystic

## The mystery of silence

Silence dwells for each of us,
subtly relates in simple ways:
peaceful, at times unsettling,
indifferent, days, harmonious
in our noisy, busy world.

Stillness, serenity, quietness
serenely manifests, allows,
the presumptuous ego, self
to recede, hide, disguise,
beyond recall. Yet silence
blesses, and sanctifies the soul.

Meditation, authentic therapy,
an act of faith, inherent discipline
brings wellness, almost charity.
In obedience, sacred silence
its only line to spirit, body,
mind and heart.

Healing, atoning, Jesus's spirit:
Father, Son, Vision of a holy fire.
Silent commodity, infinite merit.
Precious sapphire, selfless being.
Christ-like meditation to inherit,
Unending commodity now being.

*Pray as though everything depended on God.*
*Work as though everything depended on you.*
St Augustine

## For everything there is a season

Life is often mysterious and complex – full of questions. This is pre-eminently so in the realm of suffering and healing. We do not know why some people are healed of an illness, while others are not. In this life, we can never fully understand the nature and purpose of suffering.

Those of us who have a firm faith and trust in God must know that his ways are not our ways, and his thoughts are not our thoughts. The most comforting knowledge we could possibly possess is that he will heal in the way he knows best. One of the Bible's most profound statements on suffering is found in the Book of Ecclesiastes. In these statements, we begin to understand the meaning of 'letting go and letting God'. This does not mean a stoic acceptance of whatever happens to us. What it does mean is that only God, our loving Father, knows the ultimate purpose of events such as illness and suffering in our lives. We need to try to accept that everything is this world has a time and a purpose.

For everything there is a season,
and a time for every matter under heaven:
    a time to be born, and a time to die;
    a time to plant, and a time to pluck up what is planted;
    a time to kill, and a time to heal;
    a time to break down, and a time to build up;
    a time to weep, and a time to laugh;
    a time to mourn, and a time to dance;
    a time to throw away stones, and a time to gather stones together;

a time to embrace, and a time to refrain from embracing;
a time to seek, and a time to lose;
a time to keep, and a time to throw away;
a time to tear, and a time to sew;
a time to keep silence, and a time to speak;
a time to love, and a time to hate;
a time for war, and a time for peace.
He has made everything suitable for its time...
he has put a sense of past and future into their minds.

Ecclesiastes 3:1-8, 11

God blesses each one of us ...

The Lord bless you and keep you;
The Lord make his face to shine
   upon you and be gracious to you;
The Lord lift his countenance
   upon you, and give you peace ...

Numbers 6:24-26

## A prayer for faith, hope, healing, love

Lord, be our healing.
Give us complete assurance
To know of your power to heal
In the way you know
It needs to take place.

Help us to work in harmony with you –
Not against you.
Remove from us all that stops
Your loving power to heal.

In place of anger, hurt, bitterness,
Failure to forgive,
Fill us with love, joy, peace,
Patience, kindness, goodness,
Faithfulness, gentleness
And self-control.

Let these blessings grow in us,
Let them be the sign of hope,
Of healing, of love eternal.

We pray these precious promises,
Blessings for now
And for eternity,
Through the sacred Name
Of Jesus, our Friend, Brother,
Risen Lord, Redeemer.

                Amen

## Conversations of the heart

An icy wound of loneliness touches all at times,
brief, acute, universal, occasionally severe.
Age uninvolved, an ambience once chimes,
bypasses words, solitude engenders fear.

Stillness, silence, serenity, foreruns healing,
in many souls, induces a newfound being,
casts isolation clear, bypasses feeling.
Fear left aside, grace and hope, no hate.

Into the soul's silence the Lord dwells,
often intruded, stifled by ego's impudence.
Quietness, serenity, new forms of prayerfulness,
yearning the mind's seeking a sweet accordance.

Our conscience cries at times, warily speaks
in stillness or in peace. Deaf when dissidence
generates heart and mind, in a ritual seek
harmony and stilled righteousness.

Sacred silence, quietness, deep simplicity,
a sanctity finds with infinite ease, a holy synergy,
glorious state, found as if in heaven's wake.
Conversation of the heart: blessed, fulsome energy.

> *It takes courage to live through suffering; it takes honesty to observe it.*
>
> C. S. Lewis

## Harmony, healing, holiness

Monumentally beautiful, a resplendent voice, a sound
with crystal clarity, angelic harmony perfectly
magnify this hymn in a glorious praise which rings.

Palestrina's splendour infuses hope, healing, points to
the new Jerusalem in wonder, stems from a silent
heart - Jesus's Passover, atonement overflows.

Renaissance splendour unrepeated since that time,
unending fullness, holiness and peace reveals.
Heavenly encounter heard in this liturgy sublime.

Sacred sacrament, accompaniment to this magnificent
Passover and Eucharist ritual where the timeless meal
of Jesus celebrated since in redemptive joy within.

This ancient liturgy, real presence of my Jewish
and Christian self, it gloriously speaks ineffably,
eternally feeds beyond and above this earthly wish.

> For having created me to love you for eternity ... thank
> you, thank you ... my everlasting God.

What wonderful majesty! What stupendous condescension! O sublime humility! That the Lord of the whole universe, and the Son of God, should humble himself like this under the form of a little bread, for our salvation.

St Francis of Assisi

For the spirit you have given me ... Thank you, God ... For your life-sustaining sacraments ... Thank you, God ... For heart, mind, spirit, soul ... endless thanks be given ... For having created me to love you for eternity ...Thank you, God.

' ... in fact, the kingdom of God is among you.'

Luke 17:21

## Ministry of silence

Silence dwells in each of us
and may endear
itself in calming ways
signifying peace, anger,
at least indifference.
A rare creation in our noisy world.

Stillness, quietness, silently
manifests
itself, or is not revealed at all.
Silence allows the ego, the self,
to recede beyond recall.
Silence blesses, sanctifies,
by God's clear hand.

Meditation, therapy of faith,
wholeness, whether cured -
or not, a deep wellness sown.
In Jesus' sacrifice all are granted
a new lease of life.
For those for whom the Holy Spirit
calls in stillness and sacred silence,
God speaks to every heart and mind.

Silence, sacred precious commodity,
freely dispels through talk and sound.
In our world silence always speaks.
A precious sapphire of huge worth,
A selfless being is silence ...
or contemplative prayer,

whether for body, heart,
spirit, soul.

*We need stillness and silence to be able to touch souls ... to be able to hear ourselves ... God is the friend of silence.*
Mother Teresa

*In silence, God ceases to be an object and becomes an experience.*
Thomas Merton

## Our intimate reality – prayer

Mystery shrouds life, it flows from divergent
sources, manifests itself strangely,
while harm emanates from the worldly self,
causes havoc, perplexed existence,
unique oddities in every soul.

Goodness, evil, circumstance at times,
thoughts, encounters, history perhaps,
whatever route assails, God' presence
at times in a mysterious way,
in each step of life which seeks.

Our lives are more than they might appear,
we struggle to live, to love, to work, to play,
often blind, deaf, beyond the pale.
Angels secretly sanctify our days,
as Christ in love invites us to obey.

Earthquake, wind, fire touches every soul.
Rich, poor, whatever race, without control,
it matters not: God's blessings still fall.
Redeemed, forgiven: the lost, the saved,
wonder if justice truly spent.

Wholesome faith, the fullest love of Jesus'
atonement, simply like the sacrificial
Lamb allows healing for every heart,
whose spirit speaks of love, grace,
peace, though sometimes lives apart.

Precious quality, truth instils faith,
through word and sacrament forever
found. Kerygmatic, total reality, spiritually
born in humility, encounters salvation,
full and free: now, throughout eternity.

> *'How will a person brought to birth and nurtured in a world of small horizons rise up to the Lord, if you do not raise him by your hand which made him?'*
>
> John of the Cross

## The heart of all things

Crucified, conquered, his nearness above the sanctuary,
infuses depth, piety: Jesus' body freely stands,
the Cross, broken behind him, indicates love, grace.

The Paschal Lamb, atonement, salvation, showed
by these outstretched arms, mysterious wonder
embraces all: this actuality of Jesus' sacrifice.

Untold glory, redemption here revealed,
this life-like image, Jesus outpours eternal
peace. Resurrection at hand, his body sealed.

Adoration, worship, reverence here portrayed,
wonder of God's love touches every heart,
mind, spirit, soul: this image casts fear aside.

This immanence invokes silence, prayerful thought.
Jesus' presence this work of grace, of wonder casts.
Indwelling Spirit: such magnificence caught.

Living presence, sacrificial hope, reality of history
invites all who seek this awesome love.
Hope eternal in the sadness of humanity.

Incarnation, crucifixion, sad irony for Israel's history
now pleads with those who view this death, fear,
cast aside, in this everlasting victory.

> In him we have redemption through his blood, the forgiveness of our trespasses, according to the riches of his grace that he lavished on us.
>
> Ephesians 1:7

*If something does not give birth to humility, and love, and dying to self, and godly simplicity, and silence - what can it be?*
   John of the Cross, *The Ascent of Mount Carmel*

## Heart and voice sing shouts of joy

Gloriously layered polyphony, beautiful liturgical harmony,
illustrious music ignites both heart and mind, this tone,
a glorious spiritual need whose sacramental plea
obeys God's voice here in total tenderness.

A *Missa Papae Marcelli*, from little-known Palestrina,
who composed this Mass announced forgiveness, mercy,
love, peace, joy and endless praise as the soul surrenders,
a touch sublime, this music forever sings in glory.

Kyrie, Gloria, Credo, Sanctus, Benedictus, Agnus Dei.
Lamb of God whose life, in exquisitely elegant
Sounds can speak to any soul, quietly, intimately heard.
Sanctity, holiness echoes through word and sacrament.

Wonderful praise bursts in this almighty homily
of love and hope, where wholeness shows,
unites mortality within this lordly family,
surpassing the mind ... which forever flows.

Magnificent celestial sound, vision of the kingdom,
arrival in the new Jerusalem, eternal dominion
found, from this transient life, this leaven for mind,
heart, spirit, soul, surrenders all to heavenly splendour.

Awesome, yet mindful, heartfelt melodies here praise
Jesus, our risen Christ as grace produces this Passover
bread, manna from heaven: his death, resurrection
true mystery, sacrifice here infinitely portrayed.

## 102 Healing through...

Perfectly layered polyphony, glorious melody, choral sound to ignite
emotion, spirit, spiritual tone blesses heart and mind
...

## A holy moment*

When striving ceases, when ego dies,
When only praise and alleluias rise,
When I awake on resurrection's morn,
When I shall glimpse that glorious dawn.

Then I shall see my master's face
And stand in his amazing grace.
Unceasing love forever free -
It is this Lord who died for me.

A holy moment that will be,
Sheer ecstasy to be set free
From tyranny of self, from fear
And doubt, anxiety ever near.

A holy moment that will be
To meet the angels and to see
Loved ones from this veil of tears,
There to dwell beyond all years.

No more hunger, no more thirst,
Then the last shall be the first,
Then this puzzling tapestry -
Profound in its eternity.

A holy moment that will be!

---

* This poem was written in a spontaneous act after I had received a medical prognosis which limited my life to a few months. Healing at that time was not an option. That medical prognosis occurred well over twenty years ago.

## A prayer for protection

The Light of God surrounds me.

The Love of God enfolds me.

The Power of God protects me.

The Presence of God watches over me.

The Mind of God guides me.

The Life of God flows through me.

The Laws of God direct me.

The Power of God abides within me.

The Joy of God uplifts me.

The Strength of God renews me.

The Beauty of God inspires me.

Wherever I am God's presence is with me.

(This prayer was written by James Freeman for his soldier colleagues during World War II. Its power is as powerful today as it was in those distant days.)

## Prayer

Prayer the church's banquet, angel's age,
God's breath in man returning to his birth,
The soul in paraphrase, heart in pilgrimage,
The Christian plummet sounding heaven and earth.
Engine against the Almighty, sinner tower,
Reversed thunder, Christ-side piercing spear,
The six days world transporting in an hour,
A kind of tune, which all things hear and fear.
Softness and peace, and joy, and love, and bliss,
Exalted manna, gladness of the best.
Heaven in ordinary, man well rest,
The milky way, the bird of Paradise,
Church bells, beyond the stars heard, the soul's blood,
The end of spices; fomenting understood.

George Herbert (1593-1633)

*For by our nature, our will wants God and the good-will of God wants us. We shall never cease wanting and longing until we possess him in fulness and joy. The we shall have no further wants. Meanwhile, his will is that we go on knowing and loving until we are perfect in heaven.*
Julian of Norwich, *Revelation of Divine Love*

*Lay all your cares about the future trustingly in God's hands and let yourself be guided by the Lord just like a little child*

St Edith Stein

## The church's given mission for you ... for me

'I prefer a church which is bruised, hurting and dirty because it has been out on the streets, rather than a church which is unhealthy from being confined and clinging to its own security. I do not want a church concerned with being at the centre and then ends up by being caught in a web of obsessions and procedures.

'More than by fear of going astray, my hope is that we will be moved by the fear of remaining shut up within structures which give us a false sense of security, within rules that make us harsh judges, within habits which make us feel safe, while at our door people are starving and Jesus does not tire of saying to us, 'Give them something to eat'.

'The church, as the agent of evangelism, is more than an organic hierarchical institution; she is first and foremost a people advancing on its pilgrim way towards God. Excessive centralisation, rather than proving helpful, complicates the church's life and her missionary outreach.'

*The Joy of the Gospel in To-Day's World.*
(*Evangelii Gaudium*, Pope Francis, 2013.)

## A prayer for the fullness of healing

Lord, be our healing, in faith and in true reality; give us complete confidence in your almighty power to heal in the way you know it needs to take place. Help us to work in harmony with you, not against you. Remove from us all that obstructs your loving power to heal. In place of anger, hurt, bitterness, failure to forgive, fill us with Love, Joy, Peace, Patience, Kindness, Goodness, Faithfulness, Gentleness and Self-Control. May these virtues of compassion, mercy and love grow in us and be the signs of our healing in body and spirit. We pray this in the name of Jesus, our Risen Lord, now and forevermore.

# Acknowledgements

*Love, Medicine & Miracles*, Bernie Siegel, MD, selected extracts, pp. 177-179, Arrow Books, London. *Wholeness Magazine*, Healing Order of St Luke, New Zealand, 2008; *Wholeness Magazine*, Order of St Luke the Apostle, Melbourne, 1998; *A Celtic Prayer*, David Adam, *The Cry of the Deer* Triangle/SPCK, London, 1987; In Christ Alone My Hope Is Found, *The Book of Common Praise*, Oxford University Press, Melbourne, 1959; *Prayers of Life*, Michel Quoist, Gill & Macmillan, Dublin, 1969; God's Love Is Unconditional, *L'Osservatore Romano*, 16 June 2017; Rome.

The following poems were originally printed in *Good Spirits*, Paul Kraus, Michelle Anderson Publishing, Melbourne, 2014: Meditation; A Holy Moment. The verse, Healing Is... (From *Wholeness Magazine*, Healing Order of St Luke, Melbourne, 2006) was first reproduced in a *Cancer Pilgrimage, From Fear To Hope*, Cancer Monthly, Inc, North Carolina, USA.

www.ingramcontent.com/pod-product-compliance
Lightning Source LLC
Chambersburg PA
CBHW011953090526
44591CB00020B/2747